Eye of the Hare

JOHN F. DEANE was born on Achill Island on the west coast of Ireland in 1943. He founded Poetry Ireland – the National Poetry Society – and *The Poetry Ireland Review* in 1978, and is the founder of The Dedalus Press, of which he was editor from 1985 until 2006. In 2008 he was visiting scholar in the Burns Library of Boston College. John F. Deane's poetry has been translated and published in France, Bulgaria, Macedonia, Romania, Italy, Argentina, Slovakia, Serbia and several more countries. His fiction has been published by Blackstaff Press in Belfast; his most recent novel *Where No Storms Come* was published by Blackstaff in 2011. He is the recipient of the O'Shaughnessy Award for Irish Poetry and the Marten Toonder Award for Literature. He has also won the Premio Internazionale di Poesia Città de Marineo, the Ted McNulty Prize and the Gregory O'Donoghue International Prize for Poetry. He is a member of Aosdána, the body established by the Arts Council to honour artists 'whose work had made an outstanding contribution to the arts in Ireland'. His poetry has been shortlisted for the Irish Times/Poetry Now Award and for the T.S. Eliot Award. In 2007 John F. Deane was honoured by the French government by being made Chevalier en l'ordre des arts et des lettres.

JOHN F. DEANE

Eye of the Hare

CARCANET

First published in Great Britain in 2011 by

Carcanet Press Limited
Alliance House
Cross Street
Manchester M2 7AQ

A CIP catalogue record for this book is available from the British Library

ISBN 978 1 84777 092 9

The publisher acknowledges financial assistance from Arts Council England

Supported by
ARTS COUNCIL
ENGLAND

Typeset by XL Publishing Services, Tiverton
Printed and bound in England by SRP Ltd, Exeter

For Laura,

Catherine & Mary

Acknowledgements

The Furrow, *The SHOp*, RTÉ *Sunday Miscellany*, *Poetry Review* (UK), *PN Review* (UK), *World Literature Today* (USA), *The Warwick Review* (UK), *Harvard Divinity Bulletin* (USA), RTÉ *Living Word*, *Image Magazine* (USA), *The Irish Times*, *Southword*, *Temenos* (UK), *La traductière* (France), *The Forward Book of Poetry 2010* (Faber, 2009), *From the Marrow-Bone* (Columba Press, 2008).

A limited edition book, 'Achill: The Island', was published by Red Fox Press (www.redfoxpress.com) in 2009.

The Poem 'Shoemaker' was awarded the Gregory O'Donoghue International Poetry Prize 2009.

Some of the poems appeared in *The Wake Forest Series of Irish Poetry*, Volume 2 (Wake Forest University Press, 2009).

Contents

One

Two

One

Travelling Man

I was sitting in the waiting lounge, watching out onto the apron.
There were, as usual, works,
men in hard hats, yellow orange blue, with trucks and JCBs and such

chaos everywhere you would wonder if there could be
anyone in charge.
An Exxon Mobil aviation-fuel truck went by;

I heard its thundering through the thick-glass window,
felt the floor
shuddering and I thought

of the earthedness of islands, of grandmother kneading dough
for her apple and blackberry tart,
a small flouring through the hairs on her arms. Thought, too,

of the island crossroads on a Fair day, loud voices greeting,
animals skittering, the agreeable
racketing of hooves and cart-wheels across the tarred road;

left, to Keel, right to Achill Sound, long silences between passings,
and the sea, in the near distance, sounding.
Here, in Heathrow, Terminal 2, an organised confusion, an all-ways

drift and hurrying, chattering, baby-cries; alarming
head-shapes and body-forms,
children calling out in babelish grunts and noises;

left, to Athens, Düsseldorf, Algiers, right
to Munich, Sibiu and – later – home.
Then I was thirty thousand feet above the fields and towns of
                                                    Europe,

on a pitted and upflung untarred highway of air, the craft
pitched to left, to right,
like the twig I floated down the drain after a heavy

summer shower, and I thought once more of the hold,
the bold solidity, of islands
for how can you forget the sea

sounding perpetually within you, its lift
and fall, its lift
and fall, for I have come from far from such earthedness

where you may go down through layer and layer of man-bone,
of fish-bone, fish-clay, shale and scale,
from the washed-out dust of mountains, down to original molluscs

and the shaking fingers of the God.

Public House

It stood, discreet, amongst honest houses,
porter barrels tolling by the wall outside; within,
a flagstone floor, a fudge of smoke and hawking,
the round man behind the bar taciturn, graceless;

mother said it was the heaving weather of original sin
drew him in, for we are transients, pilgrims, falling
to our knees at times before unholy shrines. Began,
for him, as a faltering of resolution and he ducked,

disarmed, into the darkness, as the will falls
like a green bottle smashing itself against the flags.
But there were times, countering it, he crossed
the highest furrows of the mountainside, hunting

for goat, its wild slithering, its grazing; the bullet
in the flesh–flank of the beast was a love–song
and a gesture of despair. He stood to watch
the richening gold–light on the corrie hill,

a heaven–beam, Genesis–feet, that moved across
the mountain-side; and stood to listen to the gulls
in the next–door harbour at their disputations
speak the week's histories of calamitous events:

the tarnished china of a sheepskull and the windy
acres of its eyes, the battling through against harsh days.
Thislife, say the gulls, is that unstable province
where we scavenge behind the trawlers' arabesques,

while the human dead are taken down
into the heaving, unlit corrie
of the waves, where they fall, disarmed and slow,
down, down out of all weathers, down, like seeds.

Shelf Life

From a side-hook in the pantry, *Old Moore's*
Almanac for 1943, its pages browned from the pipe-smoke
of Grandpa Time, and one china cup without its handles,
a small blue boat drifting towards the bridge; one

Knock-shrine mug, repository for two brass keys
that have lost their locks; a brawn-coloured oval
roasting-dish, its cracked-over surface criss-crossed
with the trackways of old Europe; a Rowntree's Cocoa tin,

its comely maiden watching out onto hurrying time
with a face of wonder; a carriage clock without its hands,
standing in its final after-tock; Hallowe'en tin rings
without their lustre; a Brigid's Cross, the rushes dried

brittle as old wicks; and there, in a cardboard box,
the mixed-up bits of Lego, Meccano, jigsaws, those
building blocks of a world to be. Two off-green, birthday
balloons, wrinkled and out-of-breath, string still knotted

like scarves on their scrawny necks, and there, on the top shelf
my tinware porringer from lunchtime school, long emptied
of my peaceful indifference to all things. Finally, me, here
mooching about in my ghosthood over shelves no longer there.

The Marble Rail

I came up against the marble rail, carrying
a weight of Latin and other mysteries: men
on the left side, women on the right. I got down
to studying heads of horses on the women's scarves,
how big men knelt, one knee down on cap or hanky,
left hand to the jaw, eyes loose, fingers twitching.
There was acknowledged presence of a people's God,
snuffling, reticent, unwilling and cajoled;
I took the strange moon-bread they fed me
and turned a half a century down the aisle
to where I still attend, waiting among a frail
seniority of old Ireland, and the blood of the God
has the savour of vintage sherry and His flesh
is a melting of ashes across the tongue.

The Tombs

for Fred Marchant

We came then, Fred and I, to squeeze our spreading flesh
through an iron stile into the field;
sheep and fattening lambs shifted uneasily, their droppings
everywhere in grass;

a chaffinch-song came criss-cross from an ash;
the mound, at Dowth,
has long collapsed, stones hauled away for shed or byre;
there would have been, perhaps, a boulder

drawn across the entrance to the tomb,
now only iron grilles and rusted locks,
the shaft within disappearing into darkness,
down amongst the long-lost sons

of gravity. The poet, out of Boston – its high-rise, its interlacing
under-passageways for trains –
sent photos home by cell phone, to Arlington Massachusetts,
questions again of light those stone-age

great-great-grandfathers of ours might have known as fire,
their task to heave up stone on stone
as if the source of light could be held inside a tomb, released,
say once a year

like cattle out from the hot stable-reek onto bright pastures;
initials, near illegible, though chiselled
onto coping stones, have been dusting away for centuries
back into the air we breathe.

On the Edge

i.m. Gerry O'Malley

In retrospect
there was a tenderness to the day,
a delicacy in the midst of dread;

in the year's completion –
hydrangeas soggy brown, the plum tree branches
black and brittle – there were yet

clusters of snowdrops
as in the blest beginnings while the wind
spirited signatures across the rancid grasses

and playfully
erased them. The winter day
stretched clean and bright, the coffin came to rest on spars

over the deep-dug grave
like a new ship waiting to be launched.
In retrospect

there was a homeliness to the field
in its cold purity, while a train went by
beyond the trees and a plane rose, shimmering,

into the bluest sky.
We were holding on to the last prayers,
to the better memories, to the harmonies of wreathe

and bouquet; I thought
of last night's waking, only his face
visible above the lace and silk, like a mild

Quixote
or a Frans Hals *grand seigneur*. Now we were
holding on, the gravediggers waiting patiently

nearby. Then
he was lowered, the wilful rites
completed, we, with the brute and idling earthedness

standing numb, complicit
in the necessity of things. A flight of wood doves
passed like an exhalation over our heads, the wings

applauding loudly;
and there was order everywhere. In retrospect
there was something beautiful to the day. And unacceptable.

Still Life

for Michael Schmidt

The generations have been slipping by here
scarcely noticed; the trees we planted,

oak and birch and eucalyptus,
scarce reached our knees those days, now they rise

stooping amongst scattered stars, against
turquoise deepening to blue-pink, emerald, cobalt.

We know, after the old folks with their hearth-music
abandoned us, generations are layered beneath, and still

the young hare leaps in the joy of morningflush
while the mismatched mistlethrush will cock

her speckled chest into the northern breeze,
as it was, we say, in the beginning.

I will turn soon into the broth of dreams,
blue-pink, emerald, cobalt, a blade of grass

of being, but for now I hold my hand
against the sky and watch a star

between my fingers, see the webbed flesh, feel the blood
pulsing, and listen to the soft sigh lingering.

Bats

The untamed prairie of the stars
is shivering in evening breezes; bats come,
small scraws of blackness flinging across the dusk;

they celebrate their own
cacophonies, in a register so high it hymns
beyond human hearing; against the darkening woods

they fly, swift as thought,
precision instruments of their innocence,
feeding, as we do best, on the invisible. Before dawn

you can hear them
settling back in their attic spaces, a furred
gossiping and shouldering, the sound of a long

communal sigh;
we know they are gathering in a hot
down-side-up clustering and lustiness, clinging fast

above us who shift
in our separate togetherness,
settling on the troubled marlpool of our dreams.

Eye of the Hare

There! amongst lean-to grasses and trailing vetch
catch her? – vagrant, free-range and alert;

I saw the eager watch-tower of the ears, I knew
the power of legs that would fling her into flight;

concentrate, he said, and focus: you must love
the soft-flesh shoulder-muscles where the bullet bites,

caress – and do not jerk – the trigger: be all-embracing, be
delicate. I had no difficulty with the saucepan lid

down at the end of the meadow, lifted, for practice,
against the rhododendron hedge, I could sight

its smug self-satisfaction and shoot a hole
pea-perfect and clean through. Attention to the hare

left me perplexed for I, too, relish the vision
I imaged in its round dark eye, of a green world

easy under sunlight, of sweet sorrel and sacred herbs –
and I turned away, embarrassed, and absolved.

Cedar

In what year of war did Jehovah
abandon them? A man
riding a Yamaha XS 400 model 1982
has taken his two daughters from the ruins of their house,
has left the battered bodies of his wife and mother
among the rubble and tries to flee
across the baked, beloved fields of Lebanon —
into a hole somewhere, please God, the two
children, terrified, big eyes filled with tears, fingers
gripping hard but the bike will scarcely move, it sputters, skids,
one child before him, one behind, both tied to him
with light-blue clothes-line round their waists, the bike
slithers out into the day and turns, please
God, north on a cratered road, the sky itself so beautiful, such
an immaculate creation, and the children's voices wail
louder than the stop-go reluctant coughing of the bike
till an Israeli F16, inaudible, well-nigh invisible, so high
above, oh God please God, draws
a gash of fumes across the sky
and father, daughters, bike explode into shards
of flesh and chrome and are lost
in the bleak inheritance of the Old Testament
while only the back wheel of the bike
a Yamaha XS 400 model 1982
spins in uproarious speed and will
not stop, will not
stop

The Disappointed

And in the dream thousands of young
women and men were wading slowly out

into the lake, the bottom-mud sucked them
further and further until they disappeared

with that soundless howl possible in dreams
though audible day by day around us,

here, in this country, and now, at this time.
Can a poem touch on the soul of politics? Can it tell

how the blood-sheen on claw and bill of the chough
is beautiful beyond their machinations? Do they know

how good it is to sleep by an uncurtained window
while the dark side of the mountain looms as guardian

and a high star shades from gold to turquoise-white?
Can they bring the scent of heather, of the warming bog

into the chambers where they hurl lies and accusations
across our hurting spaces? The Christ, the poem says,

waltzed across lake water, is alive,
in light, and stone, and bone

and do you hear Him? You the anointed of the people,
the disappointed, the disappointing.

Who Have Gone Before

I see them in their ragged, glad processions,
their bodies broken, passing up the long lane,
stumbling between the ditches, joyful, and fading
into the blackness of the forest trees;
who threw off everything that I strain after
as if it were all trash and arrogance. Now
primroses already in the ditches, green knife-blades
of daffodils lift through the frozen soil; I have prayed
to saints and martyrs, to the vulgar prophets, remote
familiar figures in the extravagance of their faith,
who breathed out thanks for excruciating
agonies: Augustine, Xavier, Joan – yet the way
the blackcap bullies in around the birdfeed
and gangs of long-tailed jittery tits come
swissing through the bonebleak apple trees to seek
sustenance, then pass indignant into February grey –
leaves me again bereft and at a loss for words.

Song of the Suffering Servant

for Siobhán Dowling and Fiachra Long

Call me Princess, Sarai; I was beautiful, but barren.
I have been long uprooted, following my man,

old Abram building altars and always heading south;
I have suffered him, his mumbling to himself, taking

his mutterings as gospel. Times we pitched a tent
in the shade of the terebinth and I mingled resin in the wine

to take away the bitterness; it is no small thing the people
turn away from God, he said, my own people

moiling in darkness in which they live while the earth
falls away from them, bit by grit by bit, into blown dust.

To walk in quietness through the sand is to hear
the shush shush shush of the suffering soul;

I am a stranger on the face of earth, I live
in tents; daily I accuse myself, of unfocused longing.

I quiver, resentful, when I feel old Abram growing bitter
as lime or lemon, fidgety for children. A son, he said,

no mention of a daughter, (oh yes I would have liked
a daughter); he never spoke, but he glanced blame

at me. Sarai. Old lady. Barren. Came that day of haze,
Abram sitting idle under his oak tree, three

strangers lifted like spectres from out the sun; I saw
small disturbances of sand-dust and something stirred

uneasily within me; three male strangers, grave of face
and I knew (my man, big-husband, doing his big-man thing

again) it would mean pain for me; God does not shift
soul-spaces without purpose and the weight falls,

as it always does, on God's most loved, on woman.
I made bread for them, apricot cinnamon cakes

but they ignored them in favour of burnt flesh; men! I heard
child-promises and I giggled at the designs of God.

Now I have learned: wonders may be found in a dull place
and terror is possible in the visitation of strangers, and of God

the Creator, who laid the heavens out before her
like a camel-hair nap, in wadis, in parti-coloured fields.

Old Abram took my son away to kill him, muttering again,
taking his mutterings as gospel; I grovelled, this is bone, I said,

of my bone, blood of my blood. When they came home, chastened,
I knew I was to be (God help me!) mother of all the faithful.

Chewing on Stones

I have no words of prophecy nor augur, no strict
definitive formulae,
so when I sit to write you will only hear
commerce-noises from the street outside, the creak, sometimes

of branches stretching in the wood of the chair,
my writing hand
shifting across the page, a sound
like slow exhaled breathing –

the voice of one crying...

and, scarcely, the flowing of dark ink along the nib
like a murky water running deep,
stones within, word-stones, though, unlike the Baptist's,
of stuff that melts into the flow. I pause

to maunder out the window, trees bare yet, though holding buds,
see my own face, uncertain, puzzling.
The Baptist stood alone,
out at the edge of things, as if he would be poet –

the voice of one crying in the wilderness...

chewing on stones then spitting them out
amongst the people, the river
streaming by; desert should be the place
for such a skin-scraper, the voice prophetic

not heard against the commerce-music; the struggle
is with the ego, composed
of the most sensitive carapace, most brittle
body-parts and soul-bones;

there he may chew upon the guilt of living,
as if the dance of flesh were crime merely, as if the God
had nothing lustrous in her giving, nor any loving graced
with unconditional abundance.

the voice of one crying in the wilderness,
prepare ye the way of the Lord...

Lives of the Minor Poets

They, too, have stood, smitten and bemused,
angered at the violence of kings, caught
between a rock and the roiling ocean, between the glimpsed

shadow of a retributive deity and the gentle features
of he-who-is-to-come; they would fasten down
the voice they hear calling to them, though they know

there is no voice, only that salt
catching of pity in the throat, that coiled-fist
striking for justice that hardens the stomach's pit.

The citizens build new monuments and tall glass towers
to mirror the marching past of immaculate
manicured armies. The minor poets

fling their hands up in their rage before they pass
into the ringing silence of the Good Book; all you hear
is a contented humming, like bumble-bees

busy among the brambles on a summer afternoon:
Obadiah, Zacharias, Micah and Malachi,
Habakkuk, Zephaniah, Haggai and Nahum.

Abundance

Over the surface of the hillside,
its crannies, its low-slung water gullies,
there is a lemon-yellow glow, like light, like pollen-flush;

you and I
have breathed together such abundance
as if it were the music of a slow, profound love song,

have stood side by side, calmed
by the sheltering dimness within a stand of pines.
Once I climbed, letting my fingertips poach on pine bark and take

the teardrops to themselves, and grow
sticky with the life-sorrow of tree. This, too,
abundance. Remember those ordinary men – heavy-fleshed

and leather-handed –
who were taken out of ordinary day
and heisted into the texture of the wonderful,

wishing there would never be an outcome:
James, Peter, John… yet how they missed
the caulking of heavy-keeled boats, the gutting of fish;

they, and all of us (ah, my dear)
will stride into the welcoming arms of mercy
that day we soar off grandpa earth to take a place, living,

among starlight. The word *shrive*
touches on it, the way old grumpy Abraham
hauled himself on high along the rough-hemp rope of his faith.

Two

Edge of the Known World

Hours they spend, stitching nets along the quayside
these slow warm days; it is a time

to cast into the light such gobbets of wisdom
the older ones have harvested; time for the young

to offer mockeries. It seems they have been
forever sitting there, baiting words; their lives

are complex interactions of rope-lines
with small squares of air, that their days may hold,

that bounty be a little more assured. All this
at the earth's edge, the old unyielding ground

asserting ocean's limitations, one eye on the hemp, one
on the fluidity and refusal of the sea. They knot

patience and hope together, the windy
vowels of their humour and spittled consonants

of their expletives. In that place where Christ walks by
and throws their consciousness into chaos with his demands.

Paris

for Françoise Connolly

The city, seen from this height, lies still,
a mere, its surface scarcely stirring; as we descend
I watch a flight of doves over the waters, down
over the Panthéon and Sacré-Coeur and St Sulpice;

beneath the placid features of a face
disturbing currents;
under the New Testament, the Old;
under the new skin, the jaded.

Under the hard-sheen forecourt of the bank
there is friable earth; in the columned portico a man –
or something like a man – wraps himself round in cardboard
against another night; his this-time duvet against chill

has been Amontillado sherry and a supermarché
plastic litre bottle of almost cider.
In the shade of autumnal plane trees a group
of the elderly make, in hesitant rhythms, shapes

to hold soul and body in equilibrium; leaves
in the Jardin du Luxembourg are crumpled-paper gold
and joggers make grit-and-pebble-shuffling noises
as they pass. The old man who is out-and-down

has closed his eyes against the world, earth beneath
juddering with the haste of Métro and RER, the sky
twinkling with 747s. On the toy lake a child
sends a toy boat out with messages to the future.

Under the violent heart of Yahweh
the compassionate heart of the Christ;
under the Old Testament, the New; under the jaded skin
the fresh, and under the shaken hand the poem.

The Colours

These the colours of the seasons: gold
for the portal flowering of birth; violet

for shy kisses in a shaded copse, for days
of fast and pleading, for the iris of Van Gogh;

rose, for one long day of joy, for the survival
of sea-thrift on a famished cliff-face ledge;

suburban avenues will be clothed
in the alb of cherry-blossom white;

white and gold the chasuble
of the chestnut tree, and white

for angels flying in to the festival of snow, for virgins
crossing all together the frozen ice-paths of the Alps;

red, for martyrs, for the late-year standing of the dogwood,
the gift of tongues, the long delay of Good Friday

and the blood-stained building blocks of Gaza;
green, for the ordinary days, *de tempore* labouring,

for past time, in-between times and times ahead of times;
gold again, for the mind's embossed

portal to the sacrament, and black
for the peaceful, the having-come-through, dead.

The Colliers

They are born again out of the ribs of earth
to stand a while, stunned by light, have crawled
on bellies down constricted tunnels, along the guts

of the underearth, have struggled with the dark
implacable rock, dusts of a sojourn in the depths
tickling their throat. They are astounded once again

by gladioli, those upright, delicately blotched
ciboria of light, though what they are in need of now
is a draft of beer and a sluicing-down of flesh,

coal-dust gritting tide-lines along the bath.
Sunday they will kneel, awkwardly, at marble rails,
eyes shut, palms joined, black under the fingernails;

the immaculate hands of the priest will place
white bread on their tongues, and blood of the risen Christ
will wash through them, back into the veins of earth.

The Colliery

They closed the colliery, putting full-stop
to a dark page. They had gone down into black earth
in search of light and warmth, ingesting cold

and clothed in darkness. Their slender picks
were fashioned like those delicately nibbed pens
with which we scratched our first letters onto slates,

C for cat, for coal. On their foreheads, fixed, a third eye.
Aeneas, Dante, Hercules, went down anticipating
certain return but these, like Orpheus, found themselves

doubtful of success; here was no option for caprice
nor the exercise of pure reason; to survive
was to become like matter, so to lift again towards light.

They planted dynamite, like seeds, the mountain
rumbling in sudden pain, and some apologised each time,
for being human. Now they are learning words again,

names for stars in the black sky, for blue on the sloe's skin,
for rust on the swallow's throat. Wondering, as I do,
if anything in the world will ever wash us clean.

Words of the Unknown Soldier

He stumped us, this Jesus of yours, with his
walking on water, fandango, entrechat, glissade;
birthing, imagine! in a dark cave, out of all knowing; then

he walked the hard-baked earth of Palestine, but not
as you walk, or as I, for behind him the healing flowers grew,
the rosebay willowherb, chamomile, the John's wort;

we noted, too, that he could walk through walls,
appearing suddenly in the midst of folk as if
he were always there, waiting that they might notice him;

oh yes, this too, he walked on air
leaving them gawping upwards as he rose
higher and higher, like a skylark, walking

into the invisible. That was later. But humankind
will not be cheated of its prey for we claimed him,
hailing him fast to a tree, that he could not move

on water, earth or air, and we buried him in the underearth.
Where, it is said, he took to walking once again,
singing his larksong to the startled, to the stumped, dead.

Down to the Shore

St Mary's Abbey, Glencairn

After years of dedication they will crochet
white-wool cardigans, as if anticipating
stiff onshore breezes; will sit at ceremony,
suffering the cracking of joints or pressure of blood

against the brain; eyes no longer held in check
they watch, without blame, motions of the younger,
whose small self-conscious figurations strain,
like sailboats out on demanding seas;

they have been already, the weary ones, beyond
thresholds of endurance and have settled
here, on the ledge, old shore-birds, waiting.
Sunlight comes through the keep windows,

the walls glisten a moment, lacquer on swept
scallop shells, and they have no more questions
nor any answers, though at times they can see again
the grit road to the shore, skirl of blood-red skirts,

tossing of chough-black hair. Was there, in those days,
a figure fidgeting in the laneways, were there deep
excitable voices calling? Instead they sought,
among high marram grasses and round the cold

stone passageways of the abandoned fort,
shadows of the beautiful foreigner who passed
quick as a breeze across the anchorage, their pleading
echoes of the seas' pounding, eyes wet with tears.

Sissie

Goose-woman, ragged-haired and lone, in her thatched
half-tumbled cottage on the riverbank, her flock
a white-feather blizzard of coming-at-you scolding, and swallows

skimming the water; thick-booted and beyond age, moonlight
it was whispered, brought her, crooning and rocking, to sit
under the arch of the bridge, a small leak

from the original gutters of chaos dribbling down
into her brain. She rambled to church each Sunday, an off-kilter
beret clutching her head; she knelt, in quietude, and shared

with the rest of us, communion bread. I fished her river
for trout and ran when she, too, was a coming-at-you
arm-flailing blizzard by the stream. When the grey-lag came

low through a chilling winter dusk, honking, wheeling
down through difficult passageways, they settled, welcomed and
stilled a while, on the black pool beyond Sissie's door.

Roots

Midsummer now, too soon; on the downward slope
you are gathering speed. You have come, after so long,
to know how you should live, and there is left
so little time. Like the too-short showing of perfection

of the bearded iris: you, too, have flowered and already
the shivering has begun. The ageing bones grow brittle,
you hear them – distant wind-chimes – make a discreet
music. Rain now, midsummer, all-day rain,

slippering through the foliage; you can almost see
the runner beans stretch fragile fingers upwards
towards the roots of rain. Poets have been asserting, yet again,
the demise of God, world-maker, while you still reach

towards the roots of faith lest the human spirit droop
saturated through by the demands of physics. God's
motions: raindance on the motorways, slip-jigs, high-steps;
a slug in its ecstasy is trailing down the Matterhorn

of the whitewashed wall and you stand, awed once more,
– while the grace-filled sycamores have their green hair washed –
among the every-morning miracles, weed and seed and fruit
as the fierce, the human project hurries, unhumbly, by.

Shoemaker

He sat, cross-legged, on a deal table
as if dropped, ready-made, from an old myth;
sat, all hours, all days, lips pursed and fingers
deft and fast, like the poet

who could see the world through a needle's eye,
difficult though penetrable, a shifting, leathery mass
that might be shaped to something
beautiful, and lasting. Like the itinerant Christ

walking the ranges of Galilee, nowhere to lay down
his head. When I conjugate
Christ, and longing, what I mean
is the lake behind the cobbler's house, its waters

soothing us constantly across the night;
I mean trees, those summer mornings,
standing high and stilled within their being; on wilder days
the winds make shapes amongst them,

ghosts visiting the house, composing
their wind-leaf harmonies: I want to be able to say, again,
Christ. Our island shoemaker
sat, sometimes, outside, half-concentrating, half-

watching people go the road; he was one
in a guild with swallows and the blooming of the haw,
one with the people who went measuring their steps
in to the small chapel to divine their living, who watched

snow falling, visible through the stained glass windows, flakes
that could be birds migrating, butterflies, or spirits
out on spirit escapades. When I write
cobbler, last or nail, or when I scribble

wine, or bread, or music, what I am stitching for
is Christ, is how love still may permeate
the rush of trucks along the motorways, spray
rising against the windscreens, the wipers sighing.

Almost

Shapes of mist form among the olive trees
    and dissolve, back into darkness; almost
    dawn; impossible to know

if these are presences, or absences, the shape
    of the hewn tombstone being dominant,
    its knuckled surfaces,

its angels and stone protrusions. If you make enquiries
    as to the bodies moving through the dawn, do not expect
    answers; what is to happen

has already happened, and will go on happening
    under light's constancies, inconstancies,
    uncalled-for though declared, the ground

you walk on and the hope to which you hold. Something
    has begun its ending, and some beginnings
    will no longer be.

The Garden, Waiting

We are written down under the skin of the world
as cloudbones manuscript the skies;

we are written, too, into the drills
of underwater kitchen-gardens, where we gaze up

towards the many-jointed shoals jittering above us.
Among nightmare predatory shapes, and among

the lurking abrupt murderings where blood
drifts like smoke and dissipates, the Christ

comes beckoning, ghostly figure among ghosts.
There will be a gathering of bones, picked to a sheen

and laid jostling together, that have waited, as the heaped
bones lay, in Auschwitz, along tainted air,

waiting, in patience, for re-assemblage, waiting
until the murdered Christ at last

has gathered himself together out of the tomb
and stands, astonished in the garden, waiting.

Shorewards

The sand-and-grit-rough track curves down
towards the pier; so many dead have passed this way
I had to lean forward to bear their weight.
Life, in Old Testament weathers, scalded them,

sea – beaten by Atlantic storms – whipped sand in
till flesh was scoured from their bones
and their dry-stone houses fell to sand-mounds;
sea-flesh nourished them, barnacle, dulsk, their middens

dense with oyster shells and many-coloured sea snail whorls.
Here the mountain stream, in its peat-brown flow, touches
against the rising tide, there is a tea-black pool
silvered by the rare balletic leap of a sea trout.

On the coast road I passed, slowly, the children's graves,
wrapping myself against saltsea breezes, ageing.
On the darkening pool the swans, irritated
by tick or insect, shook their bodies to a contained

snowstorm and dipped under the surface, flapping great wings,
like prophets in a rage of warnings. Dusk came,
a bitter-apple green darkening on the horizon;
so many dead I leaned forward against their weight.

The Hare

for Pádraig J. Daly

I stood, a long while, under the arms of the eucalyptus,
its nervous leaves all

biscuit-brittle, bark lifting off in strips, one space
of isolation when your being

shifts out of dailiness and focuses onto absence.
A wood dove in the nearby grove

cooed with monotonous insistence: *tolle lege, tolle lege,*
as if the world were little more

than pages to be held up to the light. The potched
trunk of the eucalyptus rose,

a toffee-coloured column holding up the heavens
and I knew the weight of years

heavy on me, while the air of afternoon
thickened to the tolling of a bell

away over the emptied fields of the home place.
And there he was, my hare, my sweet

latchiko, white belly-bib and scut, the ears
like tablespoons filled up with snow,

watching, taut, so primed with instinctual fear I cried
that there be more than this,

more than loveliness and loss, cried for the ghosts
that are seeking still their ways

round the rush-thick meadows and pot-bellied slag-heaps
of old cottages

and these my cries, and the bell's tolling, were silent,
intense as the obdurate growing of eucalyptus.

Birds, Beasts and Buttercups

A chaffinch on the high-roof ridge
    sang to the asking pulse of the day;

I was scraping moss and grasses out of the clogged gutter,
    fingernails blackened with dead dirt;

in the meadow hazed across with buttercups
    cattle were lying, great raised heads chewing;

scarlet pimpernel have been pushing stubbornly
    up through the tarmacadamed drive and I felt

like one must have felt in the morning of the world, with the pact
    to tend and care, to register

the long day stretching towards a late grey light. This is where
    I would push the poem to go,

deep into woods, and deeper, into the clay's warmth,
    deeper still, where all that is living touches roots

– for the briefest moment – of earth's exposed harmonies;
    my fenced world is suddenly immense and I will stand, later,

to watch stars brighten against the pine-tree tops,
    knowing I have been shriven once again, and am not alone.

World, Flesh and Devil

A breeze, with an edge of bitterness, was blowing in
off the Atlantic; an unwarm sunshine
threw my image on the glassed tide-water and my shoes

sent spitlets splashing out before me.
I stood awhile
between land and ocean and found

a small stone polished sheer by sea-breaking;
cold-white as a winter moon
it dried quickly into dullness. I kept it,

touching at times on a small heart of creation
the way, perhaps, a poem
can hold all of our story within its core. At the strand's end

cathedral cliffs lifted over the waves, the contented dead
singing in chorus while high above
white seabirds soared like sacred ghosts; a small

green tent was tucked away against a bluff and fire-blackened stones
told the old ongoing tale
of human longing. In the unseen company of the elect

I knew the white stone warm against my flesh. The poem
holds within it all sanctity and sin,
the world, the flesh, the devil; angels, too, subtle

like Satan, share that silence deep inside the stone
that gives it centre and solidity
and its exact, exacting beauty, that scarce discovered

music that waits somewhere far within. And then I flung
the white stone out against the sky;
it fell without a splash into the sea and disappeared.

Three

Between Worlds

A small hallway in a two-roomed school,
a shuffle-off and scuffling to hang wet coats,
an abandoning of marvels — sherbet, lucky-bags —
then the clatterings of desk lids, slapping of books.

I learned, early, the craft of loneliness, though at playtime
I ranged and rowdied with the rest, and was stopped,
sometimes, by harmonies sensed among furze blossoms
and the assonant humming of the bees. In the rote

of rollicking verses, the every-morning roll-call:
Seán, *as láthair!* Tadhg, *anseo!* I knew the first
echoes of a music certain in its structuring, grounded, pure,
a deep and satisfactory base prelude, fugue yet to come.

Mayo Theology

for Enda McDonagh

There were high brown candles about the coffin,
the vague gesturing of their light
imaged in the sheen on the wood; I listened, hurt,
to the ongoing jeremiads and could believe
a ganglion of devils cavorted in the air;

I had to stand outside during the services, the valley –

with its dark church rising out of a copse of alders –
being an alien place, inhabited by dark invaders;

we had to wait among the gravestones that leaned,
greening, over against one another, and suffer
the ministry of midges, their almost invisible insistence
not letting us settle, as they bit and bothered
scalp and wrist and nostril.

                                                    Nanna
on her best days, stood comfortable in her body,
murmuring as she worked, hands soothed
by flour to the elbows, relishing her skills
with potato cake, potato farl, and mash;

when Harriet Graham-Green, a widow, called
to sell black roses made of crêpe paper and blue
pipe cleaners, Nanna was gracious; sure, she said,
the Protestants now are down on their luck.
Later she sang, as the butter melted on the hot
potato delicacies:

> *Slievemore, Slievemore you are standing there,*
> *your head so high and your sides so bare*
> *some day please God you will surely fall*
> *and bury the Colony Jumpers all.*

In the spring a young man's fancy turns
to spiritual heights; Nangle, foreigner,
boasting the weight of his white beard, white hair,
came angling for souls on the western coast;

potatoes failed: but there were seafoods,
dillisc, carrigeen, periwinkle, crab; the Irish
grew lean and tough as sticks of kelp; Nangle
offered soup, a hospital, a school, and built
his ordered village, set-square-shape, buying

half the side of a hill; the old men twisted caps
in their red hands, the women smiled and tried
the Gaelic tongue; it was God, dragging them
by the arms, now left, now right. They abandoned
their crooked village, straggling away uphill
over stones and bog pools and wet turf,
carrying the ever-heavier burden of their faith
down, with faint hope, into the next valley.

Lucas Cranach the Younger painted him,
our sombre plump-faced man, who suffered internal troubles,
watching a little upwards, with curious eyes;
dear Eleutherius, shocked at our abject failure
to achieve the perfection of the Christ; Luther –

they called him leper and loathsome fellow
with a brain of brass and a nose of iron;
he was truculent, with Bible pages open to show
the history of God. Blank walls before him. Anxieties
skittering like marbles across his brain, the Christ
accusing, Hell's maw gaping.

                              Nanna
sat on the steps of the stairs, her head
hidden in her hands, her index fingers
in her ears; she hummed loudly, to drown
the rattling of thunder; the devils, she said,
are playing loose among the skillets and pans.

November, All Souls, souls like a fall of rain, upwards,
the spirits released from pain when we, she said,
go in and out the chapel doors, and say the prayers;
I heard the small-growth-rustling of her rosaries,
the beads clicked softly against the polished
wood of the pew.

                                        At last, braving Satan
I hammered on the door of their grey church,
listened to the hollow sound, like the anxious pounding
of the human heart. What then, is faith? A black
stone body, inside structured grey, with plaques
to the titled dead and the lost of many wars?

or an everywhichway Church, loose cannons, a rag-
and-bone and regimented tagglebunch, marshalled
into the corral of Rome? Wittenberg, the theses;
Dugort, the darkened graves waiting
under the drawling western mist. The fall of earth
down on the polished wood was like fingernails
fibulating in my gut; I watched
a ruly goldcrest on the old high yew, its acrobatic
busyness and mastery. Their Christmas cards, Nanna said,

                                        are robins
hopping in the snow, or horse-drawn carriages
drawing up to lamp-lit houses; they carol
Good King Wenceslas and talk mulled wine
and boxing day. The hymns they sing, said Nanna,
are square like chests of tea and go on and on
interminably; and the words they use are square:
abide, vouchsafe, and gladsome. We have cribs,

an adult baby Jesus, shepherds stunned by baroque
organs in the sky; we sing Adeste, have Stephen's Day
and three wise men come offering their gifts.

Cujus regio, eius religio, a mighty fortress is our God; faith
of our fathers – and we settle down to our polite antagonisms.

This is procession across packed dirt
(the bodies, cowled)
towards a stooping, apostolic, down-and-in

to dampness of the oratory, procession
that goes on for ever,
high over the world in an embraced, embracing grief.

A process. Eucharist. Of mourning. Of rewriting
lives on a testament of rock.
Who are become priests of stone: this, too, my body – this,

my blood. Gannets amble on the air
in the surplice-white of body, suddenly a lance-dive
until you know this, too, is slaughter, faster than stroke

or coronary, the process, (as it must) disturbing.

Fulmar soar from high-brow ledges, easy as sighing, easy
as prayer; the wind-honed, entrenched will (love
ultimately), over (with a horror of height, and the midriff astrain...)

soaring laud-birds and the far-below insistent
murmurous ocean. Through the feebleness
of faith, its febrile insistent sistings, process: half-moon

soft as a sucked host against the palate of the sky.
Where death, the stranger,
through a gritted taxing of the body, may become

a friend. You can hear them still, ascetics
who whisper amongst themselves,
amidst the glassworts and samphires, sisyphussing

up and down, death to life and back; and though the high

trail of a jet appears, unfamiliar,
not one thing has changed; it is all the ongoing
ministrations of gravity and grace, of fall and lift, of doubt... Blink!

AND erosions of the stone cross will be no longer
visible, and the chipped nails of a strained monk
are still stained black by the soil; the guttural

muttering-together of the fulmar – put ye on
the Lord Jesus – has not altered.
Black today the face of the rock, gulls, resting,

arc a language of their own in white chalk;
rock, knitted to rock, bonework
of the island, and its blood is Christ: and always

green-blue water offers its white petals, pouring cream

down the eager
slopes of the rocks;
the long back-drawing sigh, the hiss;

there is a roiling of waters
and thin carpets of soiled foam
float out; all this, you know it,

are spillings from the long
procession, bead-strings, small
waltzings on the sunlit surfaces,

it is, amongst us all, communion,
Christ-loss, absence,
the abandoned faith-yards

surviving where chipped-off steps lean out over the sky.

Sheets

When she was through with them, the sheets
roistered on a sunbright day in off-the-Atlantic breezes;
Nanna washed them, there at the lake's edge, the water
a golden brown from the heather-hillside's leeching;
she trampled them in the sandy shallows, scrubbed
with a hard red soap and trampled them again;
sometimes she sang – holding long skirts up
in both hands – an air of maiden Ireland in her pains;
she stretched them out over a rock, or floated them
over the clover-speckled grass in an easing sun;
noon-time, on the high line, they were yawls,
spinnakers or topsails, sometimes clapping loud
at unexpected liberties. When I slept between them
they were elemental arms, holding me in her love.

Riddle

She carries the racketing old ash-bucket to the pit
where she sieves out the dead day's waste and burning
through the bucked riddle, the sweet-silk ash-shuffle whispering

where the grits and black-bones, sorry, blow
in last exposure; then, satisfied, she geeshes it all
onto the heap. She kept Rhode Island Red

in a fenced-off patch of stones,
with balded grass and scratchings, food-refuse, parings, peels,
carolling her chuck-chuck-chuck towards her care;

I was taken always by their mincing, the auburn feathers
gleaming gold sometimes, wet sometimes with the stain
of emerald. She would grab one, hold it sphincter-over-head

by the yellow-leather wrinkled boniness of the claws,
and lay its neck across a wooden block; I saw the fluttering
of wings, the raisin eye wide open, till she brought the hatchet down

with a rude thud; the body flapped and slackened, a tiny rain of
                                                            blood
spattering on her kitchen apron. After days the claws
are all that is left to the riddle, gold-gleams amongst the ashes.

Weeds and Wilderness

Even today the road down from the road
is untarred, potched with stones,
and turns, eelwise, round derelict homes and stables.

A hearse, wheezing from its progress, halts
by the rusted-iron gate, and the slow
muddied stream of followers stalls

against this final obstacle.
The shouldering of the burden
becomes a balancing, quick-shuffling art;

in difficult silence you are grateful
for larksong and the scolding
key-rattling calls of the stonechats.

Older graves
gleam under sunlight where patterns of shells
speak island and an old, sea-misted faith.

Among these roods of wildflowers, weeds,
tramped grass-hung passageways,
lay him down, lay old Tadhg down

gently, big-bodied, long-labouring man
entering the wet, slicked hollowness of the earth
where he has found, at last, release.

Unseasonable frost, with iris like cheering crowds
lining the garden path. Child and mother
stood awhile, mid-morning sunshine, by the ash-pit,

flecks of yesterday
lifting on the breeze; snow had made things beautiful,
frost had made them treacherous.

She ran ahead, Sarah, booted with light; but the mother
must bear her body
cautiously, and when she slipped

on ice and fell, the thump of skull on hard ground
entered the child, with that small cry,
like a furred animal's squeal

in the teeth of pain;
she lay,
as if she would lie forever, worn by it, and wearied.

He saw a scum of yellow-green trailing weed
that weighted, alien, on the surface of the lake;

the brave, once brown-gold native waves
broke sluggishly now against embarrassed shores;

and missed how the mallard used come splashing down
deliciously on the water, and how the teal

made toy-book colouring-pictures near the reeds;
the winds came striding then off heather hills

to dance the waters into silver patternings,
the ordinary extraordinary, the Saturday everyday –

or was it just the stiffness of his joints now,
the matt-grey wrinkling of tiring flesh?

The boghole lake – matrix and fern-world
in a usual fox-den stink and darkness;
there was a fierce frosting that turned

black water to a silver white, a once-off playground;
someone threw a rock far out where it sang
a sweet saxophone note

and stayed, the ice-skin stiffening;
then they were at it, sliding,
skittering and skitting, no grace to it,

only their thick-some boots –
more used to striking sparks off the stone road – now
scutting smoke-showers of ice-splicks into air;

she was child yet, lonesome, though she turned
and gaggled with the best of them, they did
eight-hand reels to their heart's battering,

and when she fell, and lifted herself off the ice, she was
scarf-blowing, belly-huffing and for a day
the universe was hers and its hallelujah.

Landlubber, with pickaxe, shovel, spade
strengthening his bones, though the small fields

were sour with rushes and sea-salt; labour made his hands
thick, made marlpools of his eyes, his chest

tough as galvanise and his flesh
leatherbound; his sideways waddling determination

took him over hillock and tussock, árdán and gryke. Tadhg.
Each clout of pick on rock was a tick, a tock

of the world's determined dying that pulsed
in his body, his slowly flesh becoming world.

Old Tadhg's nocturne was the shifting of beasts in the hot
reek of the stables, rustling of rats in the turf-mould.

Days like that the soul, too, with its burdens
is taken by a force it has no hold on,
grey-day, and louring. Sarah, child Sarah. The man,

her father, was lading groceries, and mail,
big-muscled man, taciturn, taut,
and trundled the curragh down

from its grass-nest to slide it – tethered still – out
on the sea; waved to his daughter, cast
body and soul off from the land, the craft

taken at once and angled slowly out
into the gibbering current. Strength
is an ebbing gift in him, he works

across the imperceptibly curved
surfaces of the earth, the storm, northwards,
gathering. Dread, in the girl, gathering.

Now she is wearing
a thick, white-wool gansie and folds
her arms across her breasts to hide their swelling.

She has friends, too, her gossips, her gigglers,
Annie, Breda, Nora, Niamh... Orphan,
she found welcome in the crossroads house, she would be

maid, a do-all, stay-in, lonesome creature, but
willing. Sarah. Scarce educated, but pretty, stood
late afternoons, near the old hall, where the men pass

home on their bicycles from the pub. Pass
with a swerve and a laugh, a gossip, too, and a fear
of what they did not know, and hungered for.

He rose, languidly, along the mountain,
for-now-shepherd, wellingtons and knobbed stick

for the heck of it, his few far-scattered sheep
shifting above and the slattern-bitch alert

to scent and stirrings and the commanding voice
of big-man, Tadhg, on a skite in the highlands,

relishing the tang of bilberries, the sup
scooped in the hands from the hill's flank,

small-midge-swarms swirling round his head,
the wresting of constrained selfhood away

from amongst men. And then, evening, the sun
a huge, a cardinal red, slovenly on the horizon, a mist

lifting off the mountain's lower slopes, no
dread of assault from flesh or spirit,

so he might lay himself down in a sheep-hold
shrugged to a heather ridge, curl in, and sleep.

Thursday; afternoon off. She lay, at peace,
on the hillside, her back to a heather ridge, to watch
dragonflies, impossible darting

colours and wings, to see the cities
of spindle-leggy spiders sissiping on webs
amongst the grasses; she sucked on the wine

of bilberry, chewed on salt grass; sometimes, sheltering,
she watched the circlets rain made in pools
or dust-motes hanging against sunlight. And then,

evening, the sun a cardinal red, a mist
lifting off the slopes, she would walk
back slowly, relishing the promise of dreamless sleep.

Out on the boglands he was embraced
by silence, the distant echoing of the Angelus bell

making him bob his right knee to remember,
to thud his big fist against his chest, this

day, our bread and trespasses, this sinner...
Young man now, and vigorous, veins

pulsing with life... Sometimes he wondered
if that young man-Christ had bled hot blood

at the scrape of a rasp across his knuckles.
Relishing this sphagnum world, high-lit

by late mid-morning sunshine, its energies,
gold for the journey, chrism, myrrh...

The old man, Sergeant Ted, kept a brass key
in his waistcoat pocket for the night-time
ritualised winding of the clock, the keyhole

wide as an eye, unblinking. Then there was Missie,
humped rag-and-blanket heap
always in bed in the room beyond, that caw-voice

demanding from her darksome cave: *Sarah! Saaaaayrah!*
and Mamie, old daughter, so bent in spine her knuckles
tapped on the stone floor as she walked, skirts

dark bales of shapelessness from which she murmured
so that's the way, so, so, so that's the way.
Cousins, Big Mick and Little Mick, the latter

taller and the former dumb; a squint-eyed
rheum-eyed dog, belly to the soiled earth,
snarl-barking, poised; and she heard blood

drip-dripping, keeping time, from slaughtered sheep
hung downside-up over the bright-zinc bucket. Little Mick
scraped his bitter scythe against a whetstone –

slow-moving amongst the summer-high
rushes and thistles, and yelled across at her:
Hup there! Sarah lass! and what do you say the day?

Land where all was time, untimely, dandelion clocks
profuse against the sunlight, green slime
on the water butt, rooks dark fruit in the sycamores:

where she roamed at ease, betimes, along
the sunlit long-gone-absent
underside of the world.

Clouds lingered, as though they would cling
close to earth, making of morning

a place of mystery; webs were silver filaments
shivering on the laurel hedge; three hares went

pounding away over the shorn meadow and he stood,
Tadhg, shaken, knowing that dense wall

that lifts between us and our desires. A white sun
was sheeted behind the mist and he stood

where the dogwood leaves and branches
were turning cherry-red. By noon

the kitchen warmed to the scent of stewing apples,
the Bramleys from down by the hawthorn hedge

holding the bitterness of autumn earth, the hot
sweetness of decaying grasses. Evening,

he would sit awhile over the dead hearth, hands
on his knees, head lowered; labour only

was keeping him safe, and his love affair
with earth and sheep and cattle, he would hold his mind

clear of thought and wait, till sleep took him, the way the wildering
current slewed a curragh out and away on the sea's surface.

Bean na dtrí mbó she said aloud, each time
and laughed, each time, relishing the gloom,
the reek of cow and the snuffling sounds;

slapped the rump of the first and placed the stool;
laid her head against the heaving, closed her eyes
and entered on the ping-ping rhythms of milk

spirting from the teats down into the pail;
thought of nothing as the quietened living of the cow
touched her body into patience. Milk

she would pour into the white, scoured crocks,
and set the crocks down neatly, like demurest nuns
standing to pray the Angelus for the gifts of God.

He, on the men's side, Ash
Wednesday, the whitethorn bush of penance
blossoming; to die, he was taught,
is to melt back into clay, and clay
melts back into the spittle of God;
he approached the marble rail;
the priest tipped a wine cork deep
into a saucer of ash and pressed it –
quia pulvis es – hard against his brow.

She, on the women's side, Ash
Wednesday, the whitethorn bush of penance
blossoming... *quia pulvis es*, the priest
intoned over her and the bleak ash

brushed against her brow and left
its everlasting stain. And then,
after it all, their fingers
dipping in the stoup together, they
touched, at last, and looked, at last
into each other's eyes.

They lay a long time side by side in the narrow bed,
the ceiling above them like a stilled pool,
a silence about them that could be eternity;
his touch was light, a moth's wing brushing

across a candleflame, and when he entered her
she was surprised, as if a sudden breeze
had lifted her, bodily, off the earth,
and when he entered her, he was surprised

by his knowledge and how he was part of earth
suddenly and shuddering, both of them
visiting a profound and electric darkness
from which they might not return, nor want to,

how the wild geese come each winter
down out of the coldest sky, how the cat's fur
shivers with silver lights if the finger's touch
is soft. They sat quietly then, in the kitchen,

in the scent of bitter apples stewing, with butter
melting on potato bread and spilling
to the edges of the blue plate where figures
walk forever across a stylised bridge

out of known country into unknown,
watching each other, wordless, in a dream of peace;
and later, only the smallest residue of blood
startling her, like the whispered thank you. Thank you.

Old Maud counted and separated the eggs,
the browns, the whites, the mediums, the large –

spat on them each and fretted them clean with a rag;
the small she reserved, for him, and for herself;

a soft-boiled two of small eggs, now, the yolk
the red-gold fullness of furze blossoms, a thin

finger of buttery toast dipped like an oar and goodness
brimming the shell, brimming the mouth with the gift

of hen and oatmeal, of pebble-stuff, soil-good and sun
and the scratching of creatures across famine fields;

contentment enough for a woman withdrawn, mother
and son and their murmuring clucking together,

rim of the world, goodness of hearth, and evening
and the whispering turves in their faithful congregations.

She undressed, Sarah, amongst
the dark-brown bracken,
the brown-gold ferns and ochre rushes;

her breasts so white, their red-brown nipples
lifting to the chill of the air: and hid her clothes
in under a fold of the hill...

They found her, face up, near the lake's shore,
sunk into the ooze so that scarcely
anything of her showed through the black water.

Front paws in the mudbank, Tadhg's young dog
shivered in misery, howled, and would not shift;
water lilies clustering displayed their swan-like

delicacy, the virgin petals, the deep-flesh green of their leaves
buoyant in the noon light; no Joan of Arc, this maiden,
no Saint of Àvila, no Norwich Dame. There was no salt

to lift her up, she was bride, unwilling,
of the freshwater gold-quick eels
that gnawed at her elbows, nibbled at her swollen belly.

They shut the coffin down and six brass screws,
shaped as Celtic crucifixes, fastened her in.
Perfect candles stood sentinel about her peace. Sarah. Sarah
that was. The priests sat in their black vestments,

solemn as herons at a river's edge,
tramped those slow, morose old stepping-stones –
Dies irae dies illa – leading into desolation; what
if we have not been forgiven for our birthing?

and then the V8 Zodiac heavyweight hearse –
black cringing animal exhausting grief, he followed
walking with the vaguely shifting ranks, each village window
curtained dark and every conversation muted;

on the last, rough-shingled path the men
shouldered the burden and he stood, Tadhg, scarce
comprehending, there at the dark hole; the Latin words
were hardly more than rooks' crawing

and when they shovelled earth
down on the polished boards the wailing
released high waves of misery and he wept, wept
to emphasise his new old place in the charnel world.

Behind the school, the lavatories, dale boards
half-hung, skreeks from the rusting hinges;
he soiled himself, in dread of stink and cess

and crept home, truant, and in tears;
a coloured, mesmerising chart of stars and moons,
the plotted laneways of their elliptical voyages,

hung on the schoolroom wall, with pastel maps
of the known world, of Ireland, Europe,
but he found no chart of his own fields and villages;

the words Mrs Kilbane wrote up in chalk
puzzled him with their relevance,
though he could write his name

in melting tar on a roadside wall;
they started him in infants, high, he was too big
for low, the sticks of crayon and the thin pencils

more cumbersome than shovels in his hands;
puzzled, too, when the priest came in to ask
which came first, the chicken or the egg?

Over the scutched field he chased hens,
he was cock-sure and crowing; Rhode Island Reds

they squawked with indignation; Lone Ranger, he drifted,
blowing the smoke from his six-gun till she called him

in for grooming: her Chick. Her Kid. Her Tadhg.
Mother, she nuzzled him, her dote, *a thaisce*,

and oh how the nude, vulnerable body was white
as she bathed him in the zinc tub by the fire,

water splashing the flagstone floor. She holds him, evening,
the sun a huge, a cardinal red, visibly sinking

on the horizon, a mist lifting, slowly
along the lower slopes, and for her there is no

loneliness, no fear of darkness or assault from flesh
or spirit, and the long night surely will be kind.

Piano

for Patricia

Sometimes the music stops, the half-
hearted exercises, scales like broken staircases –
and you notice silence behind the closed door

of the piano room; a stillness, fraught,
as if that lean, bedraggled figure
who has lifted the base of the window

and tries, drunkenly, to squeeze
his body through, was seeking an imagined
refuge, redemption even, where notes

had been innocently sounded by the child who has
turned and paled and will not fully trust again
the absolute mathematics of the scales.

Well-Tempered Clavier

Though I have practised over, time
and again, the long-distance running of scales
and the hurdles of arpeggios,

the symphony of the wild world plays on
beyond me. Like that stop
after a downpouring of rain. Drenching

the small-acre field, with around its edges
the honeysuckle trumpet flower,
and the wide-west strings of the winds. And me,

waiting. For the right sequences
of notes. For the harmonies. Sure
they will come. Certain

they will not. Though I have taken to myself
the fragrance of the slight, herbaceous
forest of fennel in the shrubbery, the leaves

of lady's mantle holding memories of rainfall
as if they were the silver blood-drops
of last evening's quiet moon, I am disturbed

by old cacophonies. By the false notes of my own
confusions. Watching that pendulum swing, in tempo,
shy of it, willing. Still practising.

Bikes

At the crossroads a big, joint-squealing gate
leads from the back yard to the road, an opening
out from the known world. Neighbours came
to leave their high-framed dray-horse bikes
slouched to the wall inside the gate, and took the bus
to their destinations. We assumed free rein
and took to pedalling round the yard, the bikes
bucking like jittery donkeys at our hands. But oh
how we raced, wee riders, relishing all the while
a watchful guilt, a boldness always on the point
of tears at a gashed knee or a sideways fall
into a tangle of chain and handlebars. We earned
accumulated secrecies when the travellers returned
puzzled at fine-groomed bikes standing to attention.

Ever This Night

for Herbert Lomas

There was a rose-petal sky all evening
showing from clouds that were turf-shaped and dense;
a full moon lifted behind the pine-grove and four
whooper swans flew low towards the lake,
crying, you would think,
for the familiar wastes of Iceland. I tucked down
into the warmth of the big bed, rosary beads
still curled about my fingers. I thought
how the angel would guard me across the ocean floor
of the night – then wondered, what would my angel do
in her boredom, pent in her God-given cage
of air: be watchful lest I slip into some crevasse?
or step towards the maw of a leviathan, great white
or giant squid? I drifted, bemused
that an angel's bones might be coloured
moon-white, star-blue? Feathers colour-patterned
like a goldfinch? Sleep, then, like high tide settling,
I was carried away, sails billowing, to find myself
down amongst the old and harmless wrecks, great
grandfather Ted, great-uncle John. All through the night
I was island, wide spaces opening
off every degree of the compass, life before me, its scenes
already melting into air, into thin air;
and came awake next morning, safe, and dry,
colour-patterned seashells in my hands, like dreams.

Footfalls

It is April,
    dry and hot as summer;
        wisteria languishes
like an overdressed society dame
    at a chamber concert, and purple tulips
        speak of cemeteries and sex;
in Montparnasse
    tourists have a field day,
        avenues and alleyways laid out
as rationally as an old faubourg;
    the dead
        putting on a show,
the living
    sauntering by as if nothing mattered, not
        now, perhaps not ever. Here
is Brancusi's kiss,
    womanman embracing
        as if to cleave forever;
Sartre and de Beauvoir
    have nothing new to say
        though finely suited businessmen
pass by with cameras.
    Listen to that chuckling sound –
        Saint-Saëns at it again,
doodling notes that touch
    on the bones of sunshine,
        piccolo-runs like tickled trout
finning their way towards death.
    But we have come
        for Beckett,
to stand in numb and silent thanks
    that someone led us to the edge
        and did not push,
though he impelled himself beyond the limit
    and told us of it.
        No ego-surfeiting. No longer
waiting. Move
    softly by. Like leaf-fall. Like echo's bones.
        Samuel, *salut!*

Midsummer Poem

for Gerard Smyth

These are the grey nights, high tide, high summer.
Ash-trees in the hedgerows are stirring in the mists
and you can see the fields laid out in shifting patterns;

somewhere in the night a cow is lowing, sorrowful
as a distant foghorn; dreams are disturbed, something
gleams a moment and will disappear, like a sea trout

rising, like a distant phosphorescence; breezes
that come shuffling through the alders are the breathing
of waves against a strand; no need to fear

ghosts of your loved dead who go drifting by, offshore,
their dark sails holding; the Joseph lilies, the white
Canterbury bells, hold within them, as you do,

their own light and though they will sink through the rough
autumn days, as you will, they have worked wonders
and will resurface, firmer in themselves and more fruitful.

Mimizan Plage

I know the meaning of the words: *hosanna* and *halleluia,*
the shout, and the long-drawn-out quavering belly-note:

Betty, who could not dance, dancing for exuberance
on the scullery table and Gerry shouting *Dia leat!*

you, on the beach at Mimizan;

porpoises beyond the waves at Keel, in slow ballet
over and under the ocean, stitching the sea to sky;

and you, on the beach at Mimizan;

Róisín, not watching, Tim watching out
as the car climbed through mile-high Italian villages;

you, on the beach at Mimizan;

jasmine blossoms, like milk-stars brilliant
against a dark-green sky, scenting the suburbs;

and you, on the beach at Mimizan, the red wine warming,
salamis, olives, rolls, and our hearts thundering.

More

for Ursula

There is more to it than the whimsy
of body or of mind. More than the quiet

of a pitch-skin curragh upside-down on stones
where wind and windlass and hawser

rust-meld one to other at the pier's end.
It approaches the heaving of the sea, even, at times

the crashing of waves against the coast
in dark-day Atlantic storms. More than the lilt

of a Brandenburg Concerto, or the shudder comes
at the perfect conjunctions of language. Near to prayer

but passing beyond. A reminiscence. A profound
expectancy. Something so great it judders

always beyond reach, the way the ocean shifts
in darkness past the strand-lights of the bay,

past the mast-bells and the wine. More than the waters
of all the oceans. The all of it. Then more.

Body Parts

In the Dark Wood

This, like every other, is a mustering
of words against gravity. When I lie, at night,
in that forest place before dreams, I urge my angel take
the night off while I'm gone; then
I spread wings, like an owl
launching himself from a branch, and drop heavily
onto sleep. Daylight again, toes cold on the dank moss
of the floor, body dulled with weight, I pray her
be again my guardian, envying
how she must be hoverable, how her perspective
must be lit from within, herself a clearing, and how all day
I will ignore her labours. However, if I unearth
fresh words and hear them lift off this white paperscape, then
I have a victory and am winged stone, as of Samothrace.

Sketch for the Statue of a Slave

The monastery gifted him cadavers, he would sculpt for them
a body crucified, shaping the cavity of a chest
strained into contortions, the scaffolding of the ribs
skewed against awful suffering; he had learned how the belly
is rounded out, and would sculpt a Bacchus, grapes for hair,
the flaccid serpent-stump yet idle, or cherubs
ripe with wisdom, and pubescent; marks of the chisel
a fleshly signature; awakening slave, a work
unfinished. More telling, so. Shadows are born
from the constant striking on the stone that makes
flesh flesh, and look! in spite of bone he knows
we are nursling spirits, grace-filled, and may soar;
that the killings stop, that the desecration of bodies
stop; Michelangelo has been, has left us David, the Pietà.

Body Parts

Spring-cleaning had me bitter, Cuprinol, the woodworm-whipping,
this glomerate of winter's indoor trysting, it seemed
body's strict renewal must be subjected to the flames;
I thought, Savonarola, looking mother in the eye: the monk
piqued by the power of his predictions, had wielded
words and metaphors like varnish-scrapers, like ammonia,
battering the grateful ears of his parishioners, urging
bonfire of the vanities till they took him, too, into the flames.
Later, there were retreats, custody of the flesh, the spirit
set to range through desert spaces. I chewed on the dust of zeal,
renounced, for hours, harnes of the world, and after
whaled into good food and spread the body out in luxe.
I painted the scoured-deal fireguard with curlicues of leaves,
with butterflies to gorge themselves on the nectaries of flowers.

The Caves

Dark house among outhouses, cavernous; only coal-dust
left, coal-grits, detritus; stone walls and rafters black
with dust, with cobwebs and the husks of flies. Coal-crumbs
dug through my soft soles, I touched a nail in the door
and it fell into iron flakes; the window was glaured over
and everything smelt fetid. I stood in my own darkness
within darkness, one hand in my pocket as if I had lost
something; I touched – fire. A rat lay flattened
as an emptied purse, teeth bared in hatred; I swept
coal-bits and shavings into a pile and kicked the corpse
against it and, with the lighter, tried to cleanse; flames threw
blood-coloured paintings on the walls, claw, fang and tusk,
Lascaux and Altamira, showing how in caves, *Homo erectus*
painted fear, by firelight, as if his art could save him.

Wings

Because gravity will have been dispensed with
even wings on the cusps of the shoulder blades
will not be needed. Because time will have been discarded
you will find yourself where you wish to be before
you wish it. What, then, of the pleasures of journeying?
of whiskeys and lobsterflesh? Good nights such notions
humour me, on bad, they lie more bothersome.
In the early years, sitting absently, and drifting
to the rhythms of lake water, the call I heard – *John,
follow me!* seemed seasonable; now I pray, backwards
and forwards into dimness, my body stiffening the way
slaughtered eel-bodies stiffened by the shore, my spirit saddens
into the shifting radiance on the waves' surfaces, the subtleties
and body-needs of the risen Christ merely exasperations.

Snow

for Bob O'Neill and David Horn

The pines stand high, spectacular in snow;
morning I took the Jesus Body on my tongue
tasting like a flake of snow that thawed to body-heat;

in the Burns Library, Boston College, I held
and turned, shyly, the vellum pages of a thirteenth-century
manuscript Book of Hours; roll-call of saints, *ora*

pro nobis, the pages stiff, the clasps undone but oh!
the colours: lapis lazuli and poppy red, pinheads
of gold; illuminations, the Jesus Body, long-necked birds,

the vines. I heard the young scribe breathing, I knew
the must of celibate, the dedication. Snow fell outside
and the world hushed and I heard slow footfalls

at a great distance, watched long quilled fingers reaching:
in principio, I read, *erat Verbum*... And did he pray, as I do,
that when flesh falls from bone the way soft snow

dribs from branches, that soul might melt back
into the Christ? Like me, he sat up, sometimes,
to touch his stiffening back, to gaze, in snowlight,

down the unlit tunnel of the centuries where he sat
scribing, where I sat shyly down to read: *labias
meas Domine*... A small pool had gathered

from snow melting off my boots, but I came out
at evening where the sky – lit by aurora
borealis – was cleansed by a searing frost.

Dusk

It was April, but a late March hare was shadow-boxing
with the evening moon,
there, on our front lawn; I envied him, big bucko, my sweet
latchiko, his out-there

otherness and plantedness, the phrase *hoc erat in principio*
hanging on my mind.
High in branches of the ash trees, finches and chiffchaffs
chorused, a team of long-tailed tits

came by to scold the big-limbed loper, who sat, quietened now,
priest-like on our grass. He sat alert,
some moments of composure in the good air, land lord
and local hero, his living

close to the bone, in a certain low-mass, sacramental
intensity, lest there be
fox-eyes widening from a covert or the baleful muzzle of a shotgun
poking from a hide;

he moved, mincingly at first, then sped, surefooted and at ease
back into his secrecies,
leaving me in confirmation with the earth, glad that I could face
the going down of the sun in sacred company.

Four

Achill: The Island

Gob an Choire: The Sound

Translation: mainland to island, island
to mainland, a venturing forth, a crossing
home; the difficulty, the delight

and, in the in-between, that freedom
before bridge-building, transfer
from primitive to sophisticate; small

whorl-citadels of the lug in muddy sand,
limpet-thickened rocks and witch-hair
wuthering seaweeds at low tide,

periwinkle, anemone, crab in dribble-places
at the boulder roots; challenge
of the rush of current, the whole Atlantic

pouring through towards the north, all Blacksod
emptying towards the south: the chortling
bleak heart of matter, bones of salt water,

of the flat-faced gurnard, whirlpool, eddy,
man-swallowing gorge of ocean, gob, and strait,
sceadamáin, gurges, sund.

The Major

The rhododendron wood is tattered;
in the island dispensation the Major,
scion of the reach of Empire, was hidden

from the roads, as if a modern Caliban
skulked, though a grim carriage might emerge
cautiously, to oversee, or to evict;

our people gathered hosanna blooms
for translation of the Sacrament, processed
around the chapel Corpus Christi day,

calling on Jerusalem to praise the Lord; the Major
knew the irritation of small flies
across his wood; we knew his ego-sequestration

from the crumpled poor, from curragh fishermen
and unintelligible shawled women. He died
and his effects were auctioned: gilt mirrors, chandeliers,

antlers and skulls of creatures said to come
from foreign parts, Borneo, Kuala Lumpur; now
the ragged trees are whispering a different tongue

across the breeze while a violence of starlings
swings into dusk from a sudden shout.
Protestúnach, Caitliceach, the rhododendron woods.

Sraheens: na Sraithníní: Small Holms

There is a story within the heart
of every story, its bed-rock, its sea-bed;
turn left, holding to the coast, the narrow sound

taut as a fjord between the island and the world;
at your left shoulder the small fields, the turfstacks,
self-justifying hens with their stalking cocks; geese,

custodians of the lean-to hedges, the bed-spring gateways;
the road lifts slowly towards the low hills, the quarries,
big-rock outcrops, bracken-lovely lower uplands.

There is a need always to justify the effort
of the journey; holm oak, *Quercus ilex*, something like
the glossy leaves of holly, blood-berries and a fall of catkins

bitter as tiny yellow grapes; we know
that the winds of a long affliction
can gnarl the heart, yet can you see, now can you see

the near-blind teacher walking from the Sound
uphill towards the school? The children
tease her, but she gathers them too into the story

as she has gathered the dimming light of the years
to the tapestry of her mind; she will have them read
the 'Song of Hiawatha', as if exotic strangers

tapped on the misted pane; she does not grieve,
she will walk home, black beret askew
on her cloud-wisped hair, will sit

alone in the too-hot kitchen, listening
to the sweet song of the tea, listening
to the earth about her translate its turning into sound.

Derreens: Small Woods

Step, now, out of the way, over the side-drain
into Derreens, small woods, with the wren
noisily twisting the locks on his tiny secrets;

soft rains will be moving through the branches,
their rustlings, their whisperings, and a blackbird
will sing passionately of the fall of night;

small, scurrying and several-legged things
burrow in leaf-fall and seed-cache; there is wind
forever blowing down from the Atlantic, that brings

rough news of a weather beyond the green
shelter-belt of this staid society: that the raptor
is hovering above, that the Christ has filled us full

with darkness; between the thin boles of ash and alder,
the known world (busybody sliming through) and the unknown
leave much to be desired and yet we, too, in the dance

of light across sparse woods, will find ourselves
free to gather, if the heart is open to it, the sweet
night-scented blossoming, the light the stars throw down.

Cloghmore: Big Stone

As if this were Indian territory — begins
the heathplain: browning pastures of the mountain
that sometimes fire with a violet heatherglow

down to a buffalo-coloured wild-rock seashore;
coves for the Atlantic pounding, for fat pollack
heavy as stones to pull out of the surf; turf-coloured

land-shelf for the wrecking of armadas; sky
big enough for the gannet, big enough with space
to close off the Americas. Prairie, stone place

to be grounded in, nor bush, nor scrub, the dried-out
pellets of sheep droppings scattered in the lowgrass,
the fife-whine of wind-music in the overhead wires,

the long-held low notes of the trombone
down off the lonesome slopes, the croak, too,
of raven and skald-crow and the pipit-squeak

of stare and sparrow, under the high-riding
watch-keeper hawk. Where then is the beginning
of island, and where its end? End and beginning

are one, here, Cloghmore, big stone, perpetual
god-roar of creation and, in rock-crevices, patient
in its littleness, the violet flower-head of the thrift.

Bunafahy: Lower Grassland

She was always old, grandmother, and sea-sorrow
had made her so; arms akimbo, she leaned back
against sun-warmed rocks, tired in black,

as the rocks are; easy waves came reaching
onto the strand while children's calls were lost
in the cries of gulls; a patch of the high field

glistened under sun, as the world offers, betimes, small
glistenings of joy though there are shelves of tritest stuff
no tide will cover; pulsings in the water of unwarranted

jellyfish, as if the ocean pulsed itself to pain; sister death –
idling almost visible in the rough waves offshore –
was close to her as her two lost sons, her fingertips

bruised from too much telling of the beads, it being sure
Jesus-Prospero had told an end to sorrow; now she watched
white ocean-fingers writing words onto the sand.

Bunnacurry

There is, always, a riverbank, a flowing, stuff
of dream-beginnings, where you fished
with hacked-off stick and twine, filched hook

and torn worm, lifting an eel that poured
like a thread of molten butter onto grass,
and you dreaded it, dreaded the squirm and coil,

how it would slime around your fingers,
so that you left it, stick and twine and catch,
riverbank and muddle-pool, and ran, leaving

a river that had become scarcely a stream
when you returned, a stream so choked with fern,
thistle and bramble-reach that you can barely see

91

a mud-dark trickle over mud-brown stones. Everything
altered, and everything the same, familiarity
offering some consolation till you grow aware

how far you've run, how little time is left. You have learned
to name things: teasel, stonechat, quartz, have brought
someone home you cleave to, reciting

the silly stories, telling the histories of byre
hill and hedgerow till you fall silent, awed
at the smallness of this living, weighted too

with its mysteries, knowing that, after all,
your words have been this small stream's words,
your flowing this small stream's flow.

The Monastery

Years ago the monastery died. Now
the roof has fallen through, dangerous beams
are slimed with bird shit and underneath

are dried cowpats, sheep-droppings, stale
odours, dark green fungi on the crumbling walls;
there is no way up to the tongueless bell

that waits for the moment of one final clang when it falls.
I stand a long while, shouldered by sorrow,
fretting for the words and firm hands

that built the foundations of a faith; the wind
of the passing of Jesus leaves the air still stirring,
while softest breathings of the Holy Ghost

rattle the steps of the staircase that reaches yet
towards the sky; here astounding news were spoken
and foreign wines as warm as blood consumed.

Crabs now, bitter, hard, litter the orchard grass
where brown-cassocked monks laughed and caught
windfalls in canvas aprons, who were rooting out

ground elder and sexual temptations; from the dairy
the chime of an empty churn startled; Angelus
rang out, lifting jackdaws from the sycamores,

and sweetest smoke from just-quenched candles
tickled the nostrils of Almighty God. I hear
the purring of pigeons like contented prayers

though in the railed-in graveyard everything
is in order, attending till the Spirit comes again,
the individual cell doors locked into great silence.

Purteen Harbour

High tide brims, and slews, and brims again
in the bow-legged harbour; mullet, shoaling,
worry the corpse of a discarded dogfish,

feathers of flesh float out and are swallowed, instantly;
everything is edgy; beyond the boulder bulwarks
Atlantic lays its troubled body out, and will not sleep;

oil slicks dally in their rainbow colourings, a dog
barks in frustration at the bead-bold eye of a gull;
an old half-decker, *The Thousand Ages*, drawn

up out of the waters, drips feathers of rust
to a half-hearted sun. And yet a little while
I am watching father step his old man's step

over the harbour wall, a grey-pouch fishing-bag
slung on his shoulder, the slender-bending spinning-rod
held as a standard high before him; he is stepping out

towards the favoured headland, out into the softest
evening, till he disappears again into the distance
where I watch myself as I go traipsing after.

Inishgalloon

I am smitten once again by the sheer
wonder of it, this humped-back island, bald
though green as Eden, with sheep

needle-pointing it, the way daisies hold
too-perfect lawns together; mutton
island; isle of sparrows, those

this-world specialists, the busiest, he
garrulous in black head-waiter bib, she
wild, his mistress-maid, their *chiss-chiss-cheep*

insisting their self-important politics; rumours
of the aptitude of island to draw you out,
the keyhole sea arch you can see right through

to the surf beyond, white-blue and precious
that will take the weight from your shoulders, that
high-rock fretfulness of self, those ego-tumours.

Trawmore: Big Strand

Breezes came skiffling
over the surfaces of the waves.
They brought messages, indecipherable, as always

a puzzlement – we said – because so beautiful;
down along the beach,
between the glistening high-reach wet-sand

and the powdery fineness of the dry, leaving
a wavering readable script of wheel-lines, foot-treads,
three children

in wheelchairs, three adults pushing;
under a doubtful sun they were dressed
in wools and woolscarves, the children's limbs

distorted, eyes fixed
on the nothingness of horizon;
there were otherlives cast high, razorshells,

smashed urchin bodies, and the jellyfish, the long
brown tentacles listless
in sand-shaped full stops and exclamation marks,

small eddies of sand
blown from the dunes with little whippets of foam
carried in from the breakers

and abandoned, to shiver a while on the stone
slopes. We stood, you and I, gazing at one another,
and if I have a question for you, then it must be this.

An Caol: Keel

Dawn, and high over the villages
a mustering of seagulls, in, I supposed, from the clarity of sea
to riddle the garbage dumps and duckpools

for scavengings; they circled, screaming, gave
encouragement to one another, like a crowd in belted raincoats
waiting for the scattering into another day.

Forenoon I stood on Keel beach,
absorbed by the rough Atlantic, how it smashed
its slow inexorable waves against the coast;

the sand was wet, a mirror
for lumbering caravans of clouds, while a pallid moon
stood over the mountains.

Evening, and a line of wrack
sizzled after tide, sea-excrement, rejecta,
the washed-out corpse of a gull

already raising stench.
Now a laid-back quarter-moon is suckled high and white,
the darkening not-yet-darkened sky holds

scarcesome stars above Slievemore
and if the ghosts are passing
down the old thorn lanes towards harbour, they too

are held in the grip of a chill and lonely fluency,
between the memory of births and labours, of harvests,
and of rest. I came to light a candle

in the dark church, a small flame, like a word that would
hold within itself the tidal pull of our beloved dead,
the bulked hills, the moon lightening the sky.

Slievemore: Big Mountain

Before the tender Jesus-God came, quizzical,
back out of the tomb, human still though resurrected,
before our fingers found a way to probe

his ghastly wounds for our forgiveness, giants
strode and fought on the slopes of Big Mountain;
we have found their graves still kempt

under giant stones, the kestrel's piercing scream
sounding above, the bumble bee gladdening
among the heather bells; beasts, we suppose,

were ranged against them, and the battles that they fought –
blood-inundated – were crushing to the flesh
as are ours; they went down, too, as we do, knowing life

a puzzlement, the only miracles they shared
were the colour-patterns shifting on the slopes, the sea's
berceuse-music from beyond the headlands,

the graced inebriation of their love-making
when a goddess-moon lay low and languid
on the shoulder of Slievemore. But now

we have a language that can sunder
the apathy of boulders, we have word of a victory
achieved, to still the blood, to move the mountain.

The Heinrich Böll Cottage

Against the whitewashed walls of the house
scarlet blinds across which sunlight
plays its shiftless games of shadows;

here the writer sat, watching through the window
the white war-horses out on Blacksod Bay, remembering
body-crushing tanks and the meres of blood;

down the road to the small harbour
the evening chills under the gouged slope of a mountain
looming beneath grey clouds; fishermen, smoking,

slice crumbs off the flesh of mackerel
to be bait for a hoped-for ray; the writer,
patient too, nods and turns, back to the desk and the strained

rifle-shot quickness of the typewriter.
Here, where nothing happens, where a ram
blunders in through a hedge and a pregnant cat

comes pleading to the back door, he is laying to rest the ghosts
that have followed him everywhere, here
where now only the scented heathers watch

through the breath-fogged window. The writer
sits at his table, smoking, knowing the human heart remains
uneasy in its faithfulness; he has found innocence

on an island in the far west, a place
constrained by weathers and the asking
of a rigorous God; this, only, this always, and always

it is too much. Later he will stand
bemused by family, beret
comically perched and braces taut, will watch his children rush

laughing against the waves, as if they
could hold the lifting waters back, as if they, innocent,
might shoulder as he does the whole world's burdens.